I HAVE TO KEEP RUNNING.

IF I LOOK LEFT, I GET DISTRACTED.

IF I LOOK RIGHT, I GET LOST.

IF I LOOK BACK, I FALL BEHIND, I LOSE MY FOCUS.

IF I GET AHEAD, I LOSE MY STRIDE.

I HAVE, TO KEEP RUNNING.

LEST THE DARKNESS OVERTAKE ME.

MY LEGS ARE SORE, MY HEART IS WEARY.

BUT, I HAVE A DESTINATION.

I CAN'T STOP.

IT DOESN'T NEED TO BE EASY, JUST POSSIBLE.

AND WITH GOD, ALL THINGS ARE POSSIBLE.

IT'S GETTING HARDER, AND I CAN BARELY BREATH, BUT YOU ALWAYS FIND A WAY, TO STRENGTHEN ME.

MY FEET THEY FAIL ME, BUT I JUST CAN'T STOP, BECAUSE I KNOW THAT WITH EACH STEP, IT LEADS ME CLOSER TO YOU.

I'M LOSING STRENGTH, BUT THAT'S WHERE I FIND YOURS.

I RUN THIS RACE, NOT FOR MY OWN BENEFIT, I RUN, BECAUSE I LOVE YOU.

I RUN, BECAUSE YOU'RE WHERE
THIS RACE ENDS.

MY BODY'S WEAK, BUT YOU
ESTABLISH MY STEPS. YOU
STRENGTHEN ME, YOU GIVE ME REST.

THE DARKNESS FADES, I SEE YOUR LIGHT, THIS IS WHY, I KEPT MY FIGHT.

TO SEE MY SAVIOR, GOD'S OWN SON,
TO TELL ME THIS, WELL DONE.

I AM DETERMINED, AND I WILL NOT QUIT!

If you would like to see more books by Tentmaker Ministries, please visit my website at Tm-Ministries.com.

www.ingramcontent.com/pod-product-compliance
Lightning Source LLC
Chambersburg PA
CBHW081011120626
46546CB00010B/3100